Tracking the Fox

Rosalie Sanara Petrouske

First Place Winner of The Poetry Box Chapbook Prize, 2022

Editing & Book Design by Shawn Aveningo Sanders
Cover Design by Shawn Aveningo Sanders
Cover Art by Amir Boucenna
Author Photo by Eric Palmer

First Place Winner of The Poetry Box Chapbook Prize, 2022
ISBN: 978-1-956285-27-7
Printed in the United States of America.
Wholesale distribution via Ingram.

Published by The Poetry Box®, February 2023
Portland, Oregon
https://ThePoetryBox.com

For my father:
Henry James Mastaw

"Father joins me, removes his shoes and socks,
our bare toes buried in icy blue.
Our laughter reaches the coyotes in their dens,
and black bears asleep in a tree hollow,
our joy even purer than the rushing water."

CONTENTS

The Medicine Bag

This is the medicine bag of my father's people.
Here a sacred Eagle feather,
an arrowhead deep within,
a handkerchief stained with coughed-up blood.
The lean-tos in this bag,
        the Island where
        his family existed in winter
        eating surplus beans and rice; an empty
        whiskey bottle, the father who gave him
        away.
                I reach deeper into old legends,
                an agate, a carved wooden boat,
                a birth certificate: his mother's
                name changed to Josephine
                Johnson instead of Helene Boissoneau.
                        Deeper, I uncover a single
                        blue bead, a straw basket, a map of stars,
                        the rape of his sister, Mary, at fourteen;
                        the flutter of a white moth's wings.
Fingers touch bone slivers, words
        I cannot pronounce, a cradleboard,
        a lullaby he sang to me
        in his native tongue.
His hands are in here, hammering,
nailing, pounding, rubbing my back
when I suffered from croup.
Here coiled in a corner am I,
while tight as a ball, my daughter bends
into a fetal curl.
I turn the bag inside out,
filaments alone
        drift down.

Mary Amyotte

A cousin I have never met
sends me the picture of a woman
in a white dress, Mary Amyotte.
With her long black hair,
high cheekbones, sharp angled face,
even in faded sepia, her skin looks rich,
dark and smooth.
Clothes hang on a line in the background,
something's cooking in a pot. I imagine her poking
the flames with a pointed stick, stirring laundry,
swirling water around and around with her hands,
circles of soap bubbles surrounding a mound of cotton:
undergarments, slips, gowns becoming as white
as the one she wears.
She wrings and twists, stirs the clothes
until the water ripples out
as if a stone were tossed upon its surface.

She is my father's sister, bone of my bone.
I feel a whirling inside me,
as I look at the lean-to shack
over her shoulder,
barred owls nesting in its eaves,
snowy chests and sharp beaks.

Her history is a constant movement to outlast
winter's icy winds, jagged hunger during
dry spells, dust blown in through all those cracks
                and chinks
that let light and frost into her two-room home.

It is summer, her feet are bare,
spotlessly clean on top,
though she stands on a mound of dirt.
I see those feet tapping to some fiddle music,
feel the lifting of one foot's toes, then the other's,
a faint stirring of joy inside her secret place.

I see her drop her long stick and dance.

We Didn't Know We Were at Sable Falls

Dappled leaves brush our car's hood.
Soon the dirt track grows narrower and narrower,
a fallen tree blocks our path, and my father stops.
When we get out, we can hear a gentle roar
above the faint trill of songbirds in branches high above.

I am so glad my mother isn't with us; she worries
about many things: flat tires, rabid animals, ticks, and weasels.
I know right now she wonders where we are
          and when we will return.
The path crawls through dense thicket: on one side,
a drop-off slopes into a bramble-filled ravine,
on the other, thimbleberries grow in abundance.
My father pauses to pick some and offers a handful;
their fuzzy sweetness tickles my tongue.

Breaking through the shrubbery, we see the waterfall at last.
It cascades from a sandstone cliff and pools
          in a bubble of froth below.
There are no signs to tell us our location, possibly the end
of a once traveled logging road unnamed on any map.

Scrambling over rock face, I kick off
both sandals and lower gangly ten-year-old legs
          into the foam.

Father never warns me to be careful of falling,
even though he knows I cannot swim—my mother's fault.
She is always afraid of ponds, lakes, streams, anything
that might drown her daughter.

Cool spray reaches my face, dampens the ends
      of each long braid.
I kick up more spray until my shorts
and white eyelet blouse are wet.
Father joins me, removes his shoes and socks,
      our bare toes buried in icy blue.
Our laughter reaches the coyotes in their dens,
      and black bears asleep in a tree hollow,
           our joy even purer than the rushing water.

The Visitor

When winter comes, I dislike the silence,
when it is too cold to go outside.
When sheet ice freezes the birdhouse's wooden roof,
even their feathers stiffen during the Great Spirit Moon.

But I will not think of that.

It's June, everything is green and bountiful
and the cardinal has returned to its leafy
perch in my garden.

The Hobblebush's white flowers blur in the rain.
Cardinal flickers to a branch, *misko-bineshiinh*,
always alert and watchful, he nods toward me.
When I move closer to the window,
he senses my presence and flies away.

I think about my sister who loved birds,
how they often came to the sill and sang for her.
The rooms of her house always alive with song.

Once I remember sleeping there,
my baby daughter curled against my side
as the dawn chorus awakened us.

Each day I put out seed and suet,
mix sugar water for hummingbirds,
search for lost blue jay feathers.

Errr-in, errr-in, calls the gray catbird,
then the robin, the black-capped chickadee,
        and sparrow join in.
Even the mourning dove coos sweetly at my back door.

Early Girls

I unbind roots,
push them deep into dirt.
Cherokee Red, Summer Set, Husky Cherry,
and, of course, my favorite, the Early Girls —
up to my elbows,
already with a yellow flower,
and a single green minute tomato, smaller
than the tip of my pinkie finger.

Sun warms bare shoulders, freckled skin
still smooth, one ageless part of me.
Somewhere there's still a memory
of my grandmother, planting tomatoes in her garden,
placing calloused hands over my own.
"Now tamp them down, like this," she said,
guiding my motions. "This is how we learn."
Even now, I still need someone to show me the way,
unsure if I am over-watering, using too much fertilizer,
not pruning enough.

Somehow though, the Early Girls always grow
taller and fuller, even bear fruit until frost.
By July's end, the first harvest already plucked
from its vine, round and rosy, still warm,
cupped in my palm,
and oh, so sweet in my mouth.

Tree Fall

Sunday mornings, Dad flipped
pancakes, filled a plate high
and poured maple syrup on top.
We lived in a small cabin
near the ghost town of Nahma,
where he cut trees for a living —
jack and white pines.

As they fell, their long limbs whispered
like an intake of breath.
When they landed, ground rumbled —
little earthquakes that caused
chokecherries to drop,
cottontails to scatter, roused pine beetles,
who searched frantically for escape,
sent the wolves howling even in daylight.
Each time, I shuddered inside —
felt my heart stutter.

But on those Sundays,
far away from the clear cut,
we looked out our window
to a winding creek.
Sentinel pines circled our shelter,
protected us from summer gales —
in winter — lake-effect snow.

Licking syrup from my fingers,
I watched my dad stir another batch,
waited for seconds.

Ice Storm

Ice cracks all night on the lake
and rain freezes upon branches
until they snap.
As I lie in the dark,
I can hear them falling:
loud explosions, then silence.
One hits our trailer roof,
startles the cat sleeping across my knees.
Howling, she scrambles under my bed
while I wait for the cave in,
but nothing happens.
Pulling my splayed palms from my face,
I hear my parents' murmurs.
Father tugs on boots
and pushes the door open.
Its jalousie window lets in bursts
of cold air as the panes rattle.
"Go back to sleep, dear. Everything's okay."

More than thirty years later, awake
at 3:00 a.m., I listen to the shotgun
staccato of tree limbs grazing
electrical wires and tumbling down,
barricading the street in front of our house.
The dog sleeps; my husband sleeps.
I kick off the covers and wait for Armageddon.

Shivering in my bare feet and robe,
I stumble to the front window where I see
red lights flashing over the snow.
Everything is dark and bright, blue shadows
on white, the sky a metallic gray
portending further devastation.
No one to comfort me — not here, not now.

[. . .]

In the morning, boughs from the white
pine scatter throughout our backyard.
One limb has sliced the fence,
bending metal to the ground.
The hundred-foot sentry lists
toward its wounded side
in the translucent light.
Holding my hand over my left rib,
I feel the destruction.

True North

In the woods, my father never needed a compass.
He told time by the sun's position.
When shadows grew long and slanted,
he still knew the way to turn
so we could find home.

We walked for miles, changed paths:
North, South, East, and West,
through golden tamaracks in autumn,
beneath old growth hemlocks, white pines,
and birches in summer.

If nightfall caught up to us, Father took my hand,
admonished me to watch for roots, burrows
tunneled into earth by badgers, woodchucks, or foxes.
At dusk, the Eastern screech owl's eerie trill
filled our ears as it swooped down from its perch
to devour a shrew or bat.

"If you think you are lost," Father told me, "travel downhill,
search for water, read the night sky," and he pointed
at Polaris perched at the tip of the Little Dipper's handle.

In daylight, he taught me why trees have more leaves on one
    side.
"To find true North," he said, "place a stick straight up in the
    ground,
mark where the stick's shadow lands with a rock."

But he was my true north, astride his shoulders
when I grew tired, I became taller than his six-foot frame.
His hands were the needle of my compass,
his voice my straight-edged arrow.

Seeking Refuge

Rain, all night, ripples over roof.
Gut-shiver cold, long-limbed pine
gale bent, slaps shadows,
against my window like reaching arms.
River rises, whispers dark,
rain and river do not speak.
In my house, alone, too many thoughts
and I cannot sleep.

My heart taps, taps with the loose shingle.
No beast is out tonight—woodpeckers, beak-silenced,
squirrel, hollow-huddled, mole, deep-tunneled.

Fist-shook angry sky does its best to frighten.
Rowdy winds bend the birch,
yet branches do not break.
No star twinkle, no wisp of light,
no promise for my heart tonight,
but its steady beat thumps in time
with the clatter, and the shatter,
the howling whooshes.
Squirrel wraps around hoarded stash.
Mole sleeps, earth-locked deep,
toes unfurled.
Tucked into their tree, woodpeckers rest
as do I, at last, blanket-wrapped
and fetal-curled.

The Sky I Was Born Under

~after Joy Harjo

The sky I was born under was directionless,
one could not tell if it was up or down —
It began with the formation of pewter clouds,
a winter storm warning,
and then my mother's labor began in earnest.
Soon the heavens spewed snowflakes
larger than my fist pushed into the space
beneath her ribcage.

The sky I was born under was wakeful.
Traveling in the warm cavern of womb,
in my ears, mother's erratic heartbeat pounded.
I leapt inside her like the snowshoe hare
as it galloped across a field,
and ducked out of sight.
My parents told me they drove for miles on M-28 —
no center line to follow.
Deer stayed hidden, as did fox and coyote,
not a time for creatures to roam or hunt food.
They tucked themselves into dens and hollows,
insects crawled under the bark of trees and made love.
Only wolf broke silence with his bawdy howls
at the angry skies before he too hunkered
down with his mate, paws tucked beneath his chest
to wait.

The sky I was born under was so bitter,
it froze the tips of one's fingers if exposed too long.
A traveler died that night when his car ran out of gas,
his body hunched and stiff over the steering wheel,
where he fell asleep before help arrived.

[. . .]

The sky I was born under was unforgiving,
my birth recorded months later, my father's race
declared as Indian by a small-town city clerk,
not Ojibwe or *Anishinaabe* — just the
harshness of "Indian" as non-entity.

The sky I was born under was also forgiving.
Two days later, on the drive back
to our home along the Adams Trail,
I slept swaddled in blankets,
my tiny palm cradled against Mother's cheek while
Father steered carefully over snow-packed roads.
My mother told me a fox crossed in front of our car,
brazenly waved his red tail,
and Father slowed to let him pass.
The ermine greeted us before he bobbed under a mound of white.
Beaver slapped ice from his tail at the river,
and a migrating flock of snowy owls landed
in a nearby birch and watched us with their wise eyes.

When we trekked up the trail to the cabin's front door,
she said a thin ray of sunlight broke through the clouds.
I wailed for the first time, my voice
ricocheted in the stillness,
and all the forest creatures paused to listen.

Tracking the Fox

In the snow there are no footprints,
at least no human ones. The animal tracks belong
to the fox Grandmother shoos away
when he creeps too close to the chicken coop.

His ruddy fur has faded, his body lanky—
there is little food this winter for the beasts.
My father has found two dead deer in the woods,
their bones sticking out, partly devoured.
Perhaps, the fox has been there; he looks healthier
        now, his sides bloated.

I follow him on my snowshoes,
over one hill, then down another
until I reach the creek where water
still trickles and hisses beneath a cracked
        sheet of ice.

Tree branches graze my face.
When I crawl under the spruce,
heavy with snow, the end of my long braid
is soon soaked through.
My snowshoes leave large, latticed prints behind me,
so I look like some dinosaur-era creature,
        feet crooked and unwieldy.

When I look back, I see only white.
I could be lost, but I'm not.
In a cluster of nearby pines,
a blackbird hurls away
causing a small avalanche.
He calls out eerily,
his loud caws make my heart quake.

[. . .]

On the other side of the creek
I see movement against rough bark,
a brief slash of red —
fox has burrowed in, his beady dark eyes
watch me — I should turn back now
before I am truly lost, but unafraid
        I stand,
wait for one of us to make
        the first move.

Squaw

The man approached me
at the Rusty Nail.
Behind him, a thin, dark-eyed woman trailed.
"This here's my girlfriend, we were sittin'
over there." He pointed at an empty table
opposite the dance floor.
"I thought you was pretty. You have
the same cheekbones. See."
He pulled the girl forward, clutched her chin,
twisted her face so the light
from above stippled
across it casting shadows
like hollow gourds beneath her eyes.
It made her prominent features stand out.
"She's a squaw too. I bought you a drink."
He leered as the bartender set the glass before me.
Heat crawled up my neck, into my face,
settled in my pores.
My brown skin, long black hair, my pride.
But like my father before me, I denied who I was.
"I'm not Indian," I said.
Squaw, the way he said it . . .
I saw the bruise on the girl's arm
when the sleeve of her t-shirt rode up,
a perfect rounded thumbprint, ripe as a plum.
Squaw, to my people — offensive, meant to belittle.
This grinning white man reminded me
of those California Gold Rush squatters,
when squaw was another label
for disrespect, rape, and verbal abuse.
He stood before me with that stupid smirk,
waiting for my thank you.
I wanted to spit at him, punch his jaw,
throw the drink in his face;
instead, I turned my back, gulped its contents,
felt the alcohol burn inside my mouth.

Eating Corn Soup
under the Strawberry Moon
(Beaver Island, Michigan, June 2019)

At the community center, they serve bowls
of Indian corn soup, fry bread and whitefish, lightly
sautéed to a perfect golden brown.
The Ojibwe woman behind the table wears jeans and t-shirt,
a traditional medicine bag tied around her neck,
long gray hair pulled back in a thick braid.

She tells me great-great-great grandmothers
handed down this recipe
to mothers, to sisters, to her.
"Grandmothers born," she said, "before even cameras existed."
She notes the camera strapped around my neck.
"It takes three days to make," she tells me,
"the corn is soaked and cooked in hardwood ashes."

I picture her sifting the ashes,
while water heats in a cast-iron pot,
using her sturdy thumb to push kernels
up and off the cob—then stirring, stirring, stirring,
waiting, waiting, waiting for just the right consistency,
tasting and then tasting again.
She talks for a long time, until the next person steps in line.
Smiling, I thank her, know she is not giving away any secrets.

I take my bowl, plate with fry bread and fish
back to the communal table beneath the stars,
drop a ten-dollar bill in the donation jar.
At the first spoonful, my mouth explodes with flavor—
smoke, ashes, salt, unnamed spices, *mandaamin*—
both tang and sweetness, such savory delights.

Slowly, I let each bite slide down my throat,
finish my bowl and go back for another,
then one more, drop more money into the jar.

Later, will be drums, sacred tobacco
offered to the night sky, along with a prayer —
I join many voices, my belly filled with soup,
and feel no hunger tonight.

Solstice

Snow blows harshly against the windows
as the tin roof rattles.
When the wind finally rests at midnight,
she opens the shade.
A few flakes skittle on the wind while a pale
moon drifts high above black limbs — solstice still.
Her grandmother's voice slips in.
"Little one, don't you know rabbits come out to frolic
in the moonlight?"
So, she watches for a long time.

In the morning, she finds a circle
of Eastern cottontail tracks
around the spruce,
they disappear under the fence
and into the woods, speak
of joyful abandon
beneath the Long Night Moon.

Before Leaving

I climb black rocks with my daughter,
who scrambles ahead.
Close behind, I'm ready to reach out
should she stumble on the uneven surface.
At the top, we stare out at Superior,
breathing in the peace of lake and sky.
Below, a few waves crest white,
then lap
the million-year-old ledge beneath us.

On a far shore, sugar maple, hemlock, balsam fir
and white pine cover the island and grow down sides
of distant outcroppings.
Pairs of seagulls rise from the Bon Rocks.
They lift and circle,
          dip and glide.
To the West, I point out Hogsback
and Sugarloaf, remnants of ancient glaciers.

Near us, a group of college students gather.
We watch as they leap from the highest point
to plummet into icy water.
This ritual repeats year after year.
Perhaps, I think, one day my daughter will dive
from this cliff into Superior's silvery-blue.
Her breath will catch when she rises
and gulps in warm air,
yet her heart will beat again
when she discovers
effortless, she can fall and still rise.

For now, we simply sit side by side.
Sun warms our shoulder blades
and dampness gathers in the hollows
of our necks

[. . .]

where tendrils of hair separate to expose
skin to mid-afternoon light.

I tell her this place, this moment will always be part of us—
its mantra will call to us when we close our eyes
and still hear lake sounds, as if someone placed
a seashell against our ears.
We will carry it inside.
"Inside here?" she asks.
She places a hand across her chest.

Reaching, I take her other hand.
I squeeze, but she pulls away.
            "Don't hold on so tightly," she says.

Leaving North

Once more I leave the lake behind, drive south
through an autumn rain—in my rear view
leaves are muted, a smear of multi-color red.
I'll miss being here for first snow.

When I was younger, I felt I'd never escape,
though now I feel I'll never be able to return.
I'll miss this sky at midnight when it flickers
with northern lights, their brilliance brighter
than your eyes.

I'll miss walking these hilly streets,
our table at the coffee shop
where we piled stacks of books:
Robert Frost, Williams and his plums,
Dickinson and her fear of death.
Perhaps, you feared it too.

I'll miss the rocks at McCarty's Cove, the tremble
of blue spruce, and when spring finally comes,
I'll miss trillium's white trumpeting
along the sides of every road.

Autumn Evening Walk

I walk through mulched leaves while the sun sets,
pink, pink beyond my shoulders.
It glows too on red berries left for the birds,
and one crimson maple that still holds tightly to its leaves.
Beneath my boots, acorns slide, twigs crackle,
then geese start suddenly,
honk loudly, their wings whir
and flutter wildly before they splash land —
a smooth touchdown,
as they glide onto the river's still surface.
And I am a motion too.
Who knows though where I will be
next year, next month, or even tomorrow?
But I am here now, walking fast,
my breath a small sigh of sound.

November 1, 2020

The last days of October
blue moon
pink-slashed sky
always those expectations
for it to be one way or another

Curled and uncurled in my fetal dark
it takes so long for the light to arrive
now
cold
still
frost embedded in stiff blades of grass
sunlight thin and wounded

Words writhe within me
what I cannot say
cannot name
tongue curled
tip sore and scalded
bitten-back hopes

Yet at mid-morning downy woodpecker
dances and darts
grabs bits of suet from the feeder
the red spot on his head
crowns morning

Found

My father walks ahead of me on the trail.
I can no longer see him in the fading light,
yet I know he's there.
Almost lost, I tell myself not to be afraid —
find the sky above towering hemlocks and white pines.
He waits at lake's edge with canoe and oars.
I don't remember him ever paddling a boat.
My mother yelled if he brought me near water.
As a little girl, a summer squall nearly capsized
her and her father on Carp Lake —
she never taught me to swim.
I step into the boat, found and safe.
As we push off from shore,
our oars glide effortlessly with each stroke,
forward through the air and backwards through the water.
The sky is spackled with stars, the Big Dipper
Perseus, Cassiopeia, and even Sagittarius stringing his bow.
Somehow, I know this is a dream,
yet I want to stay forever —
to listen to the small splashes of oar to water,
shiver in the cool breeze sweeping my forearms —
just us going somewhere.
An owl calls, a nighthawk's screech echoes,
then all falls silent.
The forest enfolds me in its breath,
fills me with the natural rhythms
my father taught me,
holds me in the arms of memory,
until I and the wild ones sleep.

A Preponderance of Rain

The morning fields are golden with soybeans.
When they lose their leaves,
the farmer gathers them.

The grass, soaked with nightfall rain, glistens
as do flower petals in the butterfly garden.
Yellow maple leaves, curled and damp,
scatter recklessly across the lawn.

This summer felt shorter than others did.
Daughter gone; time should slow —
instead, I seem propelled sooner to the end.

Between rows of soybeans,
Sulphurs flit, as if winter will never come.
Pick, gather, reap —
even the corn has taken all season to grow tall.

The red barn rests against eggshell clouds,
makes false promises.
Will the rains come again before morning ends?

I press a hand to my chest, if only this, if only that.
If I had turned right rather than left,
would I be here now waiting for the sun
to light up this field?

The downpour has dampened leaf cover.
I wear sandals on my walk,
leather soon soaked through.

It feels good, though, rhythms of crickets, crow's caws,
distant gobbles of wild turkeys.
On the ground, an iridescent tail feather,
banded with bronze and gold.

[. . .]

I collect the pieces of my wishes, a shard of blue sky,
string the chips into a wind chime
that will sing me to sleep.

New Year's Day

Sun circles our yard for a moment
making the snow sparkle, what little of it
there is, while the dog orbits its perimeter,
his small realm of acorns, squirrels,
and branches sheared off by icy wind.
The first day of this new year still holds promise,
nothing has been denied, the word "no"
not even shaped by tongues or lips.
There are other promises for this fresh-faced
time baby, other words held within
like precious seeds in a jack pine cone,
waiting for the raging crown fires
of northern summers to release them to earth.
I resolve to open my heart to pure vibrating
vowels, subjects unexplored, sentences
that will germinate once the ground cools.
Even as I write this, I feel the heat penetrating
through the marrow of my deepest bone.

To Begin Again

The whole sky is yours
to write on, blown open
to a blank page
          — Rita Dove

Red barn, rusty bricked silo,
stretched fields
across a backdrop of melon sky.
Dawn, cold, nine degrees.
Sugar maple branches move slightly
in an inhalation of wind,
black bird wings shadow snow.

White stretches over fields,
indented by deer and rabbit tracks—
they scrawl their footprints across
its surface.

To begin again, is it possible
to simply ask forgiveness
to know it is enough?

"Affirmative," nods Dried Leaf
clinging bravely to a twig.
"Yes," caws Crow,
"Indeed," bobs Cottontail's head,
as he lopes along the fence
hurrying back to his nest.

"Morning sky is yours," Crow
calls over his shoulder.
"Tell your story."

At Founder's Landing

I can do nothing about loss,
except learn from others who have also lost
places, times, lovers, those who are dear.
I can walk into the sunrise, or stroll along the lake,
smooth my hands over rock.
I can be strong as a white pine bending in a gale,
the hawk swooping down for its evening meal, the lake itself
that claims those swimmers foolish enough to embrace its
    undertow.
I could wear my losses in the creases around my eyes.
Oh wisdom, I could say, the ability to know the difference.
But can I ever truly learn? Such predictable humans we are —
always wanting the unobtainable, the unsustainable.

But I have hope that I can keep something,
if only I know how to look up or down, to breathe deeply
and hold those breaths, to inhale the fragrant pine needles
crushed beneath my soles.
Star patterns in the sky every night, milkweed on the prairie,
Monarch butterflies, fireflies, cricket songs in August.
I can learn to live with loss, let it toughen the muscles
of my heart, even if its beat skips and stutters.
I can draw a circle of protection and sit amongst the missing,
let their voices slip under my fingernails, reverberate in my
    mouth,
and echo in my ears.

Black Ash Basket

My daughter and I weave black ash strips
    over-under, over-under,
dip them in water to keep each pliable.
My fingers smell like soil, like tree.
Side by side, our shoulders brush, our hands grow
tired from pulling each section taut.

We take our place amongst generations of Ojibwe women,
who sat in circles alongside sisters, mothers, aunts.
Although, we wear jeans and sweaters,
and when we break for a meal, we go to a cafeteria
to fill our plates with fried rice and fortune cookies
from the Chinese vendor.
Our teacher is a fifth-generation weaver — she keeps
us on task, sets the rhythm,
    over-under, over-under.
My fingers smell like fiddlehead ferns, like work.

My daughter hums, breathes softly, our elbows touch.
She is proud of her creation — we shape the weave gently
between our palms so the baskets keep their form.
    Then *over-under, over-under.*
My father's mother is our blood-link.
Was she a weaver too?
Do we have her nose, eyes, or high cheekbones?
We'll never know.
My fingers smell like sweetgrass, like memory.

Our forearms touch as we reach for the last strip of bark.
    Over-under, over-under,
we are almost finished.
Born on Sugar Island on the Fourth of July,
my father's mother, Helene, died at forty-two,
no grave marker mentions women like her.

Her children left motherless, a name on a census roll.
Ancestral pain runs deep in my veins,
in waves like the big lake, *Gichigami.*

It floods in my heart, in my daughter's —
that lake of our births, but unlike those before us,
we shall let our voices be heard,
rise to speak the rape and desecration of our pasts —
and we will weave power into our baskets,
place within them flowers, pebbles, feathers,
beads aglow with light.

After the workshop,
we admire each other's handiwork,
exclaim over perfectly woven rows.
Smiling, we pose for a picture.

Our fingers smell like cedar, like hope.

ACKNOWLEDGMENTS

The author gratefully thanks and acknowledges the following publications where poems in this collection previously appeared, sometimes in earlier versions:

"Before Leaving" appeared in *And Here: 100 Years of Upper Peninsula Writing, 1917-2017*, edited by Ronald Riekki, Michigan State University Press

"Black Ash Basket" appeared in the *Southern Poetry Collective: Blue Mountain Review*, 2021

"Eating Corn Soup under the Strawberry Moon" appeared in *Cultural Daily*, finalist in the 2020 Jack Grapes Poetry Prize

"Founder's Landing" appeared in *Rejoice, Everyone! Reo Town Reading Anthology!* a collection of writing from the REO Town Reading Series, edited by Matthew Rossi, 2020

"Leaving North" appeared in *Third Wednesday*, Spring 2014

"New Year's Day" appeared in *The Michigan Poet*, Broadside, April/May 2015

"The Medicine Bag" and "Mary Amyotte" appeared in the anthology *Voice on The Water: Great Lakes Native America Now*, a collection of Native American writing edited by Grace Chaillier and Rebecca Tavernini, Northern Michigan University Press, 2011

"The Visitor," "Leaving North," and "New Year's Day" appeared in *Third Wednesday*, Vol. XII, No. 2, Spring, 2019

"True North" appeared in *Sky Island Journal*, Winter 2020

Tracking the Fox was also a finalist in the *Trail to Table* 2022 Open Reading Period, an imprint of Wandering Aengus Press, Jill McCabe Johnson, Publisher and Editor

With much appreciation for Mary Fox, Margaret Krusinga, and Loraine Hudson, along with all the other members of my writing groups who have commented on the many different versions of the poems in this collection. Your support and friendship over the years is greatly valued.

EARLY PRAISE FOR
TRACKING THE FOX

The poems in *Tracking the Fox* unfold at the slow pace of a hike in the woods, inviting the pleasures and joys of nature, while never turning away from the shared struggles and pain of the poet's Ojibwe heritage. Hers is a fearless language that holds it all, like the black ash basket she weaves with her daughter, welcoming every reader with each personal, conversational, and precise poem. This is an ambitious, necessary voice committed to truth-telling and the naming of creatures, large and small, that make up our world. In "The Sky I Was Born Under," written in homage to U.S. Poet Laureate Joy Harjo's piece of the same name, she describes the scene of her own birth, ending with the lines: "I wailed for the first time, my voice/ ricocheted in the stillness,/ and all the forest creatures paused to listen." *Tracking the Fox* will cause us all to pause and listen to the hard-won work of this poet coming into her own as a Native American woman and mother, promising: "we shall let our voices be heard."

— James Crews, contest judge
poet, editor of *How to Love the World*

Replete with the flora and fauna of Michigan's Upper Peninsula, Rosalie Sanara Petrouske's *Tracking the Fox* takes readers on a spiritual journey imbued with the presence of her Ojibwe father, her "true north" whose teachings filled her with "the natural rhythms" of the world around her. In the first poem, Rosalie Sanara Petrouske turns "The Medicine Bag" of her father's family inside out, discovering sacred objects; ancestral stories of the struggle for existence despite harsh winters and brutal racism; and the tenderness of a father's love. These "filaments... drift down" throughout the collection as the poet deftly weaves the beauty of forests and rain, sweetgrass and stars with the affirmation that comes from communal traditions and taking

[. . .]

one's "place amongst generations." *Tracking the Fox* gives us poems to read and reread, both for the beauty of their immersion in nature and for the way they help to dissolve "deep...ancestral pain."

—Dr. Terry Bohnhorst Blackhawk, author *One Less River*,
Kresge Arts in Detroit Literary Fellow

Tracking the Fox showcases Petrouske's skill with traversing poems of the domestic and natural worlds. These narrative and meditative poems remind us how home and place return to us, even after we've left. I admire Petrouske's voice, for it holds tension, making the reader eager for every reverberating, often haunting, ending. Come, listen to the voices here: a father's utterance; the all-night rain; a fox's silent slash of red; jack and white pines falling, their limbs "like an intake of breath." I tell you, with lines like "I can do nothing about loss,/ except learn from others who have also lost," this is a poet you want to know.

—Janine Certo, author of *O Body of Bliss*,
winner of the Longleaf Press Book Contest in Poetry (2022)

Rosalie Sanara Petrouske has given us a gift to savor in these lovely poems which cross over the threshold between living and actually being in the world. What she has done so deftly is to explore her connections to her Anishinaabe past, present and future, with a heartfelt look into Ceremonial time. These poems sing with the understanding of the natural world and the inner lives of things. There are direct links between wisdom, ancestry, and the lessons of simply walking the earth, knowing how to read the sky, or how to understand the talk of crows. Take them outside and sit with them and you will be all the better for it. These heal what needs healing.

—Michael Delp, Co-editor of *Made in Michigan*,
Wayne State University Press

ABOUT THE AUTHOR

Rosalie Sanara Petrouske is the author of *What We Keep* (Finishing Line Press, 2016), *A Postcard from my Mother* (Finishing Line Press, 2004), and *The Geisha Box* (March Street Press, 1996). Petrouske's poems and essays have appeared in many literary journals: *Passages North, Red Rock Review, Rhino, The MacGuffin, Southern Poetry Review, Third Wednesday, Sky Island Journal, Blueline,* and *Lunch Ticket,* among others. Her poetry was also included in several anthologies, the most recent, *100 Years of Upper Peninsula Writing, 1917-2017* from MSU Press and *Voice on the Water: Great Lakes Native America Now* from Northern Michigan University Press.

Her poem "Eating Corn Soup Under the Strawberry Moon" was one of six finalists in the 2020 Jack Grapes Poetry Prize from *Cultural Daily*. In 2021, she was one of five finalists for the distinction of U.P. Poet Laureate (of the Upper Peninsula of Michigan). Images of the natural world are prominent throughout her work as she stays true to the teachings of her Ojibwe father, who taught her how to provide careful stewardship and to always honor her surrounding environment, whether a woodland or urban landscape.

About The Poetry Box® Chapbook Prize

The Poetry Box® Chapbook Prize is open to both established poets and emerging talent alike. The contest is open to poets residing in the United States and is open for submissions each year during the month of February. Find more information at ThePoetryBox.com.

2022 Winners
Tracking the Fox by Rosalie Sanara Petrouske

Elemental Things by Michael S. Glaser

Listening in the Dark by Suzy Harris

2021 Winners
Erasures of My Coming Out (Letter) by Mary Warren Foulk

Of the Forest by Linda Ferguson

Let's Hear It for the Horses by Tricia Knoll

2020 Winners
The Day of My First Driving Lesson by Tiel Aisha Ansari

My Mother Never Died Before by Marcia B. Loughran

Off Coldwater Canyon by C.W. Emerson

2019 Winners
Moroccan Holiday by Lauren Tivey

Hello, Darling by Christine Higgins

Falling into the River by Debbie Hall

2018 Winners
Shrinking Bones by Judy K. Mosher

November Quilt by Penelope Scambly Schott

14: Antología del Sonoran by Christopher Bogart

Fireweed by Gudrun Bortman